THE MOTHER

Sri Aurobindo

SANAGE
PUBLISHING HOUSE

Paperback: 978-936205028-1
eBook: 978-936205577-4

Printed by:

Sanage Publishing House LLP
Mumbai, India

sanagepublishing@gmail.com

Sri Aurobindo (born **Aurobindo Ghose**; 15 August 1872 –5 December 1950) was an Indian philosopher, yogi, maharishi, poet, and Indian nationalist. He was also a journalist, editing newspapers such as Bande Mataram. He joined the Indian movement for independence from British colonial rule, until 1910 was one of its influential leaders, and then became a spiritual reformer, introducing his visions on human progress and spiritual evolution.

His main literary works are *The Life Divine*, which deals with the philosophical aspect of Integral Yoga; *Synthesis of Yoga*, which deals with the principles and methods of Integral Yoga; and Savitri: A Legend and a Symbol, an epic poem.

Contents

Publisher's Note

The Mother consists of six chapters, all of them written in 1927. The first chapter was originally written as a message, the second to fifth chapters as letters. The sixth and longest chapter was written for inclusion in a booklet that eventually comprised the message, the letters, and Chapter 6. This booklet was first published under the title **The Mother** in 1928. The present text has been checked against Sri Aurobindo's manuscripts

The Mother and Sri Aurobindo giving darshan on 24 April 1950

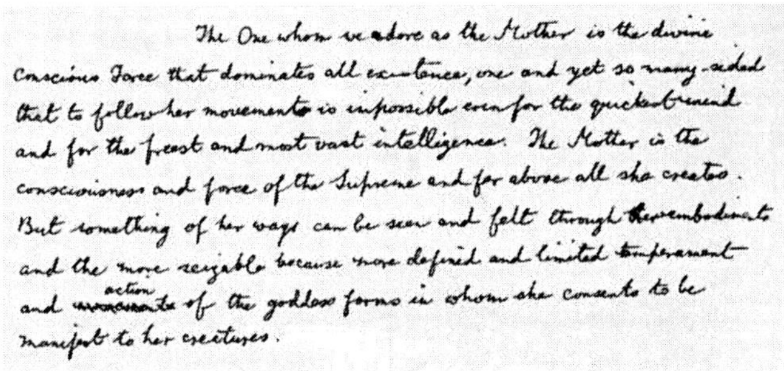

The One whom we adore as the Mother is the divine Conscious Force that dominates all existence, one and yet so many-sided that to follow her movements is impossible even for the quickest mind and for the freest and most vast intelligence. The Mother is the consciousness and force of the Supreme and far above all she creates. But something of her ways can be seen and felt through her embodiments and the more seizable because more defined and limited temperament and action of the goddess forms in whom she consents to be manifest to her creatures.

The Mother

The One whom we adore as the Mother is the divine Conscious Force that dominates all existence, one and yet so many-sided that to follow her movement is impossible even for the quickest mind and for the freest and most vast intelligence. The Mother is the consciousness and force of the Supreme and far above all she creates. But something of her ways can be seen and felt through her embodiments and the more seizable because more defined and limited temperament and action of the goddess forms in whom she consents to be manifest to her creatures.

Passage from the opening paragraph
of chapter 6 of *The Mother*

I

There are two powers that alone can effect in their conjunction the great and difficult thing which is the aim of our endeavour, a fixed and unfailing aspiration that calls from below and a supreme Grace from above that answers.

But the supreme Grace will act only in the conditions of the Light and the Truth; it will not act in conditions laid upon it by the Falsehood and the Ignorance. For if it were to yield to the demands of the Falsehood, it would defeat its own purpose.

These are the conditions of the Light and Truth, the sole conditions under which the highest Force will descend; and it is only the very highest supramental Force descending from above and opening from below that can victoriously handle the physical Nature and annihilate its difficulties . . . There must be a total and sincere surrender; there must be an exclusive self-opening to the divine Power; there must be a constant and integral choice of the Truth that is descending, a constant and integral rejection of the falsehood of the mental, vital and physical Powers and Appearances that still rule the earth-Nature.

The surrender must be total and seize all the parts of the being. It is not enough that the psychic should respond, and the higher mental accept or even the inner vital submit and the inner physical consciousness feel the influence. There must be in no part of the being, even the most external, anything that makes a reserve, anything that hides behind doubts, confusions and subterfuges, anything that revolts or refuses.

If part of the being surrenders, but another part reserves itself, follows its own way or makes its own conditions, then each time that that happens, you are yourself pushing the divine Grace away from you.

If behind your devotion and surrender you make a cover for your desires, egoistic demands and vital insistences, if you put these things in place of the true aspiration or mix them with it and try to impose them on the Divine Shakti, then it is idle to invoke the divine Grace to transform you.

If you open yourself on one side or in one part to the Truth and on another side are constantly opening the gates to hostile forces, it is vain to expect that the divine Grace will abide with you. You must keep the temple clean if you wish to install there the living Presence.

If each time the Power intervenes and brings in the Truth, you turn your back on it and call in again the falsehood that has been expelled, it is not the divine Grace that you must blame for failing you, but the falsity of your own will and the imperfection of your own surrender.

If you call for the Truth and yet something in you chooses what is false, ignorant and undivine or even simply is unwilling to reject it altogether, then always you will be open to attack, and the Grace will recede from you. Detect first what is false or obscure in you and persistently reject it, then alone can you rightly call for the divine Power to transform you.

Do not imagine that truth and falsehood, light and darkness, surrender and selfishness can be allowed to dwell together in the house consecrated to the Divine. The transformation must be integral, and integral therefore the rejection of all that withstands it.

Reject the false notion that the divine Power will do and is bound to do everything for you at your demand and even though you do not satisfy the conditions laid down by the Supreme. Make your surrender true and complete, then only will all else be done for you.

Reject too the false and indolent expectation that the divine Power will do even the surrender for you. The Supreme demands your surrender to her but does not impose it: you are free at every moment, till the irrevocable transformation comes, to deny and to reject the Divine or to recall your self-giving, if you are willing to suffer the spiritual consequence. Your surrender must be self-made and free; it must be the surrender of a living being, not of an inert automaton or mechanical tool.

An inert passivity is constantly confused with the real surrender, but out of an inert passivity nothing true and powerful can come. It is the inert passivity of physical Nature that leaves it at the mercy of every obscure or undivine influence. A glad and strong and helpful submission is demanded to the working of the Divine Force, the obedience of the illumined disciple of the Truth, of the inner Warrior who fights against obscurity and falsehood, of the faithful servant of the Divine.

This is the true attitude and only those who can take and keep it, preserve a faith unshaken by disappointments and difficulties and shall pass through the ordeal to the supreme victory and the great transmutation.

II

In all that is done in the universe, the Divine through his Shakti is behind all action, but he is veiled by his Yoga Maya and works through the ego of the Jiva in the lower nature.

In Yoga also it is the Divine who is the Sadhaka and the Sadhana; it is his Shakti with her light, power, knowledge, consciousness, Ananda, acting upon the Adhara and, when it is opened to her, pouring into it with these divine forces that makes the Sadhana possible. But so long as the lower nature is active the personal effort of the Sadhaka remains necessary.

The personal effort required is a triple labour of aspiration, rejection and surrender, — an aspiration vigilant, constant, unceasing — the mind's will, the heart's seeking, the assent of the vital being, the will to open and make plastic the physical consciousness and nature rejection of the movements of the lower nature — rejection of the mind's ideas, opinions, preferences, habits, constructions, so that the true knowledge may find free room in a silent mind, — rejection of the vital nature's desires, demands, cravings, sensations, passions, selfishness, pride, arrogance, lust, greed, jealousy, envy, hostility to the Truth, so that the true power and joy may pour from above into a calm, large, strong and consecrated vital being, — rejection of the physical nature's stupidity, doubt, disbelief, obscurity, obstinacy, pettiness, laziness, unwillingness to change, tamas, so that the true stability of Light, Power, Ananda may establish itself in a body growing always more divine; surrender of oneself and all one is and has and every plane of the consciousness and every movement to the Divine and the Shakti.

* * *

In proportion as the surrender and self-consecration progress the Sadhaka becomes conscious of the Divine Shakti doing the Sadhana, pouring into him more and more of herself, finding in him the freedom and perfection of the Divine Nature. The more this conscious process replaces his own effort, the more rapid and true becomes his progress. But it cannot completely replace the necessity of personal effort until the surrender and consecration are pure and complete from top to bottom.

Note that a tamasic surrender refusing to fulfil the conditions and calling on God to do everything and save one all the trouble and struggle is a deception and does not lead to freedom and perfection.

III

To walk through life armoured against all fear, peril and disaster, only two things are needed, two that go always together — the Grace of the Divine Mother and on your side an inner state made up of faith, sincerity and surrender. Let your faith be pure, candid and perfect. An egoistic faith in the mental and vital being tainted by ambition, pride, vanity, mental arrogance, vital self-will, personal demand, desire for the petty satisfactions of the lower nature is a low and smoke-obscured flame that cannot burn upwards to heaven. Regard your life as given you only for the divine work and to help in the divine manifestation. Desire nothing but the purity, force, light, wideness, calm, Ananda of the divine consciousness and its insistence to transform and perfect your mind, life and body. Ask for nothing but the divine, spiritual and supramental Truth, its realisation on earth and in you and in all who are called and chosen, and the conditions needed for its creation and its victory over all opposing forces.

Let your sincerity and surrender be genuine and entire. When you give yourself, give completely, without demand, without condition, without reservation so that all in you shall belong to the Divine Mother and nothing be left to the ego or given to any other power.

The more complete your faith, sincerity and surrender, the more will grace and protection be with you. And when the grace and protection of the Divine Mother are with you, what is there that can touch you or whom need you fear? A little of it even will carry you through all difficulties, obstacles and dangers; surrounded by its full presence you can go securely on your way because it is hers, careless of all menace, unaffected by any hostility however powerful, whether from this world or from worlds invisible. Its touch can turn difficulties into opportunities, failure into success and weakness into unfaltering strength. For the grace of the Divine Mother is the sanction of the Supreme and now or tomorrow its effect is sure, a thing decreed, inevitable and irresistible.

IV

Money is the visible sign of a universal force, and this force in its manifestation on earth works on the vital and physical planes and is indispensable to the fullness of the outer life. In its origin and its true action, it belongs to the Divine. But like other powers of the Divine, it is delegated here and in the ignorance of the lower Nature can be usurped for the uses of the ego or held by Asuric influences and perverted to their purpose. This is indeed one of the three forces—power, wealth, sex—that have the strongest attraction for the human ego and the Asura and are most generally mis-held and misused by those who retain them. The seekers or keepers of wealth are more often possessed rather than its possessors; few escape entirely a certain distorting influence stamped on it by its long seizure and perversion by the Asura. For this reason, most spiritual disciplines insist on a complete self-control, detachment and renunciation of all bondage to wealth and of all personal and egoistic desire for its possession. Some even put a ban on money and riches and proclaim poverty and bareness of life as the only spiritual condition. But this is an error; it leaves the power in the hands of the hostile forces. To reconquer it for the Divine to whom it belongs and use it divinely for the divine life is the supramental way for the Sadhaka.

You must neither turn with an ascetic shrinking from the money power, the means it gives and the objects it brings, nor cherish a rajasic attachment to them or a spirit of enslaving self-indulgence in their gratifications. Regard wealth simply as a power to be won back for the Mother and placed at her service.

All wealth belongs to the Divine and those who hold it are trustees, not possessors. It is with them today, tomorrow it may be elsewhere. All depends on the way they discharge their trust while it is with them, in what spirit, with what consciousness in their use of it, to what purpose.

In your personal use of money look on all you have or get or bring as the Mother's. Make no demand but accept what you receive from her and use it for the purposes for which it is given to you. Be entirely selfless, entirely scrupulous, exact, careful in detail, a good trustee; always consider that it is her possessions and not your own that you are handling. On the other hand, what you receive for her lay, religiously before her; turn nothing to your own or anybody else's purpose.

Do not look up to men because of their riches or allow yourself to be impressed by the show, the power or the influence. When you ask for the Mother, you must feel that it is she who is demanding through you a very little of what belongs to her and the man from whom you ask will be judged by his response.

If you are free from the money-taint but without any ascetic withdrawal, you will have a greater power to command the money-force for the divine work. Equality of mind, absence of demand and the full dedication of all you possess and receive and all your power of acquisition to the Divine Shakti and her work are the signs of this freedom. Any perturbation of mind with regard to money and its use, any claim, any grudging is a sure index of some imperfection or bondage.

The ideal Sadhaka in this kind is one who if required to live poorly can so live and no sense of want will affect him or interfere with the full inner play of the divine consciousness, and if he is required to live richly, can so live and never for a moment fall into desire or attachment to his wealth or to the things that he uses or servitude to self-indulgence or a weak bondage to the habits that the possession of riches creates. The divine Will is all for him and the divine Ananda.

In the supramental creation the money-force has to be restored to the Divine Power and used for a true and beautiful and harmonious equipment and ordering of a new divinised vital and physical existence in whatever way the Divine Mother herself decides in her creative vision. But first it must be conquered back for her and those will be strongest for the conquest who are in this part of their nature strong and large and free from ego and surrendered without any claim or withholding or hesitation, pure and powerful channels for the Supreme Puissance.

V

If you want to be a true doer of divine works, your first aim must be to be totally free from all desire and self-regarding ego. All your life must be an offering and a sacrifice to the Supreme; your only object in action shall be to serve, to receive, to fulfil, to become a manifesting instrument of the Divine Shakti in her works. You must grow in the divine consciousness till there is no difference between your will and hers, no motive except her impulsion in you, no action that is not her conscious action in you and through you.

Until you are capable of this complete dynamic identification, you have to regard yourself as a soul and body created for her service, one who does all for her sake. Even if the idea of the separate worker is strong in you and you feel that it is you who do the act, yet it must be done for her. All stress of egoistic choice, all hankering after personal profit, all stipulation of self-regarding desire must be extirpated from the nature. There must be no demand for fruit and no seeking for reward; the only fruit for you is the pleasure of the Divine Mother and the fulfilment of her work, your only reward a constant progression in divine consciousness and calm and strength and bliss. The joy of service and the joy of inner growth through works is the sufficient recompense of the selfless worker.

But a time will come when you will feel more and more that you are the instrument and not the worker. For first by the force of your devotion your contact with the Divine Mother will become so intimate that at all times you will have only to concentrate and to put everything into her hands to have her present guidance, her direct command or impulse, the sure indication of the thing to be done and the way to do it and the result. And afterwards you will realise that the divine Shakti not only inspires and guides but initiates and carries out your works; all your movements are originated by her, all your powers are hers, mind, life and body are conscious and joyful instruments of her action, means for her play, moulds for her manifestation in the physical universe. There can be no more happy condition than this union and dependence; for this step carries you back beyond the borderline from the life of stress and suffering in the ignorance into the truth of your spiritual being, into its deep peace and its intense Ananda.

While this transformation is being done it is more than ever necessary to keep yourself free from all the taint of the perversions of the ego. Let no demand or insistence creep in to stain the purity of the self-giving and the sacrifice. There must be no attachment to the work or the result, no laying down of conditions, no claim to possess the Power that should possess you, no pride of the instrument, no vanity or arrogance. Nothing in the mind or in the vital or physical parts should be suffered to distort to its own use or seize for its own personal and separate satisfaction the greatness of the forces that are acting through you. Let your faith, your sincerity, your purity of aspiration be absolute and pervasive of all the planes and layers of the being; then every disturbing element and distorting influence will progressively fall away from your nature.

The last stage of this perfection will come when you are completely identified with the Divine Mother and feel yourself to be no longer another and separate being, instrument, servant or worker but truly a child and eternal portion of her consciousness and force. Always she will be in you and you in her; it will be your constant, simple and natural experience that all your thought and seeing and action, your very breathing and moving come from her and are hers. You will know and see and feel that you are a person and power formed by her out of herself, put out from her for the play and yet always safe in her, being of her being, consciousness of her consciousness, force of her force, Ananda of her Ananda. When this condition is entire and her supramental energies can freely move you, then you will be perfect in divine works; knowledge, will, action will become sure, simple, luminous, spontaneous, flawless, an outflow from the Supreme, a divine movement of the Eternal.

VI

The four Powers of the Mother are four of her outstanding Personalities, portions and embodiments of her divinity through whom she acts on her creatures, orders and harmonises her creations in the worlds and directs the working out of her thousand forces. For the Mother is one but she comes before us with differing aspects; many are her powers and personalities, many her emanations and Vibhutis that do her work in the universe. The One whom we adore as the Mother is the divine Conscious Force that dominates all existence, one and yet so many-sided that to follow her movement is impossible even for the quickest mind and for the freest and most vast intelligence. The Mother is the consciousness and force of the Supreme and far above all she creates. But something of her ways can be seen and felt through her embodiments and the more seizable because more defined and limited temperament and action of the goddess forms in whom she consents to be manifest to her creatures.

There are three ways of being the Mother of which you can become aware when you enter into touch of oneness with the Conscious Force that upholds us and the universe. Transcendent, the original supreme Shakti, she stands above the worlds and links the creation to the ever-unmanifest mystery of the Supreme. Universal, the cosmic Mahashakti, she creates all these beings and contains and enters, supports and conducts all these million processes and forces. Individual, she embodies the power of these two vaster ways of her existence, makes them living and near to us and mediates between the human personality and the divine Nature.

The one original transcendent Shakti, the Mother stands above all the worlds and bears in her eternal consciousness the Supreme Divine. Alone, she harbours the absolute Power and the ineffable Presence; containing or calling the Truths that have to be manifested, she brings them down from the Mystery in which they were hidden into the light of her infinite consciousness and gives them a form of force in her omnipotent power and her boundless life and a body in the universe. The Supreme is manifest in her forever as the everlasting Sachchidananda, manifested through her in the worlds as the one and dual consciousness of Ishwara-Shakti and the dual principle of Purusha-Prakriti, embodied by her in the Worlds and the Planes and the Gods and their Energies and figured because of her as all that is in the known worlds and in unknown others. All is her play with the Supreme; all is her manifestation of the mysteries of the Eternal, the miracles of the Infinite. All is she, for all are parcel and portion of the divine Conscious-Force. Nothing can be here or elsewhere but what she decides and the Supreme sanctions; nothing can take shape except what she moved by the Supreme perceives and forms after casting it into seed in her creating Ananda.

The Mahashakti, the universal Mother, works out whatever is transmitted by her transcendent consciousness from the Supreme and enters into the worlds that she has made; her presence fills and supports them with the divine spirit and the divine all-sustaining force and delight without which they could not exist. That which we call Nature or Prakriti is only her most outward executive aspect; she marshals and arranges the harmony of her forces and processes, impels the operations of Nature and moves among them secret or manifest in all that can be seen or experienced or put into motion of life. Each of the worlds is nothing but one play of the Mahashakti of that system of worlds or universe, who is there as the cosmic Soul and Personality of the transcendent Mother. Each is something that she has seen in her vision, gathered into her heart of beauty and power and created in her Ananda.

But there are many planes of her creation, many steps of the Divine Shakti. At the summit of this manifestation of which we are a part there are worlds of infinite existence, consciousness, force and bliss over which the Mother stands as the unveiled eternal Power. All beings there live and move in an ineffable completeness and unalterable oneness, because she carries them safely in her arms forever. Nearer to us are the worlds of a perfect supramental creation in which the Mother is the supramental Mahashakti, a Power of divine omniscient Will and omnipotent Knowledge always apparent in its unfailing works and spontaneously perfect in every process. There all movements are the steps of the Truth; there all beings are souls and powers and bodies of the divine Light; there all experiences are seas and floods and waves of an intense and absolute Ananda. But here where we dwell are the worlds of the Ignorance, worlds of mind and life and body separated in consciousness from their source, of which this earth is a significant Centre, and its evolution a crucial process. This too with all its obscurity and struggle and imperfection is upheld by the Universal Mother; this too is impelled and guided to its secret aim by the Mahashakti.

The Mother as the Mahashakti of this triple world of the Ignorance stands in an intermediate plane between the supramental Light, the Truth life, the Truth creation which has to be brought down here and this mounting and descending hierarchy of planes of consciousness that like a double ladder lapse into the nescience of Matter and climb back again through the flowering of life and soul and mind into the infinity of the Spirit. Determining all that shall be in this universe and in the terrestrial evolution by what she sees and feels and pours from her, she stands there above the Gods and all her Powers and Personalities are put out in front of her for the action and she sends down emanations of them into these lower worlds to intervene, to govern, to battle and conquer, to lead and turn their cycles, to direct the total and the individual lines of their forces. These Emanations are the many divine forms and personalities in which men have worshipped her under different names throughout the ages. But also, she prepares and shapes through these Powers and their emanations the minds and bodies of her Vibhutis, even as she prepares and shapes minds and bodies for the Vibhutis of the Ishwara, that she may manifest in the physical world and in the disguise of the human consciousness some ray of her power and quality and presence. All the scenes of the earth-play have been like a drama arranged and planned and staged by her with the cosmic Gods for her assistants and herself as a veiled actor.

The Mother not only governs all from above, but she descends into this lesser triple universe. Impersonally, all things here, even the movements of the Ignorance, are herself in veiled power and her creations in diminished substance, her Nature-body and Nature-force and they exist because, moved by the mysterious fiat of the Supreme to work out something that was there in the possibilities of the Infinite, she has consented to the great sacrifice and has put on like a mask the soul and forms of the Ignorance. But personally, too she has stooped to descend here into the Darkness that she may lead it to the Light, into the Falsehood and Error that she may convert it to the Truth, into this Death that she may turn it to godlike Life, into this world-pain and its obstinate sorrow and suffering that she may end it in the transforming ecstasy of her sublime Ananda. In her deep and great love for her children she has consented to put on herself the cloak of this obscurity, condescended to bear the attacks and torturing influences of the powers of the Darkness and the Falsehood, borne to pass through the portals of the birth that is a death, taken upon herself the pangs and sorrows and sufferings of the creation, since it seemed that thus alone could it be lifted to the Light and Joy and Truth and eternal Life. This is the great sacrifice called sometimes the sacrifice of the Purusha, but much more deeply the holocaust of Prakriti, the sacrifice of the Divine Mother.

Four great Aspects of the Mother, four of her leading Powers and Personalities have stood in front in her guidance of this universe and in her dealings with the terrestrial play. One is her personality of calm wideness and comprehending wisdom and tranquil benignity and inexhaustible compassion and sovereign and surpassing majesty and all-ruling greatness. Another embodies her power of splendid strength and irresistible passion, her warrior mood, her overwhelming will, her impetuous swiftness and world-shaking force. A third is vivid and sweet and wonderful with her deep secret of beauty and harmony and fine rhythm, her intricate and subtle opulence, her compelling attraction and captivating grace. The fourth is equipped with her close and profound capacity of intimate knowledge and careful flawless work and quiet and exact perfection in all things. Wisdom, Strength, Harmony, Perfection are their several attributes, and it is these powers that they bring with them into the world, manifest in a human disguise in their Vibhutis and shall found in the divine degree of their ascension in those who can open their earthly nature to the direct and living influence of the Mother. To the four we give the four great names, Maheshwari, Mahakali, Mahalakshmi, Mahasaraswati.

Imperial MAHESHWARI is seated in the wideness above the thinking mind and will and sublimates and greatens them into wisdom and largeness or floods with a splendour beyond them. For she is the mighty and wise One who opens us to the supramental infinities and the cosmic vastness, to the grandeur of the supreme Light, to a treasure-house of miraculous knowledge, to the measureless movement of the Mother's eternal forces. Tranquil is she and wonderful, great and calm forever. Nothing can move her because all wisdom is in her; nothing is hidden from her that she chooses to know; she comprehends all things and all beings and their nature and what moves them and the law of the world and its times and how all was and is and must be. A strength is in her that meets everything and master's and none can prevail in the end against her vast intangible wisdom and high tranquil power. Equal, patient and unalterable in her will she deals with men according to their nature and with things and happenings according to their force and the truth that is in them. Partiality she has none, but she follows the decrees of the Supreme and some she raises up and some she casts down or puts away from her into the darkness. To the wise she gives a greater and more luminous wisdom; those that have vision she admits to her counsels; on the hostile she imposes the consequence of their hostility; the ignorant and foolish she leads according to their blindness. In each man she answers and handles the different elements of his nature according to their need and their urge and the return they call for, puts on them the required pressure or leaves them to their cherished liberty to prosper in the ways of the Ignorance or to perish. For she is above all, bound by nothing, attached to nothing in the universe. Yet she has more than any other the heart of the universal Mother. For her compassion is endless and inexhaustible; all are to her eyes her children and portions of the One, even the Asura and Rakshasa and Pisacha and those that are revolted and hostile. Even her rejections are only a postponement, even her punishments are a grace. But her compassion does not blind her wisdom or turn her action from the course decreed; for the Truth of things is her one concern, knowledge her Centre of power and to build our soul and our nature into the divine Truth her mission and her labour.

MAHAKALI is of another nature. Not wideness but height, not wisdom but force and strength are her peculiar power. There is in her an overwhelming intensity, a mighty passion of force to achieve, a divine violence rushing to shatter every limit and obstacle. All her divinity leaps out in a splendour of tempestuous action; she is there for swiftness, for the immediately effective process, the rapid and direct stroke, the frontal assault that carries everything before it. Terrible is her face to the Asura, dangerous and ruthless her mood against the haters of the Divine; for she is the Warrior of the Worlds who never shrinks from the battle. Intolerant of imperfection, she deals roughly with all in man that is unwilling, and she is severe to all that is obstinately ignorant and obscure; her wrath is immediate and dire against treachery and falsehood and malignity, ill-will is smitten at once by her scourge. Indifference, negligence and sloth in the divine work she cannot bear, and she smites awake at once with sharp pain, if need be, the untimely slumberer and the loiterer. The impulses that are swift and straight and frank, the movements that are unreserved and absolute, the aspiration that mounts in flame are the motion of Mahakali. Her spirit is tameless, her vision and will are high and far-reaching like the flight of an eagle, her feet are rapid on the upward way and her hands are outstretched to strike and to succour. For she too is the Mother, and her love is as intense as her wrath, and she has a deep and passionate kindness. When she is allowed to intervene in her strength, then in one moment are broken like things without consistence the obstacles that immobilise or the enemies that assail the seeker. If her anger is dreadful to the hostile and the vehemence of her pressure painful to the weak and timid, she is loved and worshipped by the great, the strong and the noble; for they feel that her blows beat what is rebellious in their material into strength and perfect truth, hammer straight what is wry and perverse and expel what is impure or defective. But for her what is done in a day might have taken centuries; without her Ananda might be wide and grave or soft and sweet and beautiful but would lose the flaming joy of its most absolute intensities. To knowledge she gives a conquering might, brings to beauty and harmony a high and mounting movement and imparts to the slow and difficult labour after perfection an impetus that multiplies the power and shortens the long way. Nothing can satisfy her that falls short of the supreme ecstasies, the highest heights, the noblest aims, the largest vistas. Therefore, with her is the victorious force of the Divine and it is by grace of her fire and passion and speed if the great achievement can be done now rather than hereafter.

Wisdom and Force are not the only manifestations of the supreme Mother; there is a subtler mystery of her nature and without it, Wisdom and Force would be incomplete things and without it, perfection would not be perfect. Above them is the miracle of eternal beauty, an unseizable secret of divine harmonies, the compelling magic of an irresistible universal charm and attraction that draws and holds things and forces and beings together and obliges them to meet and unite that a hidden Ananda may play from behind the veil and make of them its rhythms and its figures. This is the power of MAHALAKSHMI and there is no aspect of the Divine Shakti more attractive to the heart of embodied beings. Maheshwari can appear too calm and great and distant for the littleness of earthly nature to approach or contain her, Mahakali too swift and formidable for its weakness to bear; but all turn with joy and longing to Mahalakshmi. For she throws the spell of the intoxicating sweetness of the Divine: to be close to her is a profound happiness and to feel her within the heart is to make existence a rapture and a marvel; grace and charm and tenderness flow out from her like light from the sun and wherever she fixes her wonderful gaze or let's fall the loveliness of her smile, the soul is seized and made captive and plunged into the depths of an unfathomable bliss. Magnetic is the touch of her hands and their occult and delicate influence refines mind and life and body and where she presses her feet course miraculous streams of an entrancing Ananda.

And yet it is not easy to meet the demand of this enchanting Power or to keep her presence. Harmony and beauty of the mind and soul, harmony and beauty of the thoughts and feelings, harmony and beauty in every outward act and movement, harmony and beauty of the life and surroundings, this is the demand of Mahalakshmi. Where there is affinity to the rhythms of the secret world-bliss and response to the call of the All-Beautiful and concord and unity and the glad flow of many lives turned towards the Divine, in that atmosphere she consents to abide. But all that is ugly and mean and base, all that is poor and sordid and squalid, all that is brutal and coarse repels her advent. Where love and beauty are not or are reluctant to be born, she does not come; where they are mixed and disfigured with baser things, she turns soon to depart or cares little to pour her riches. If she finds herself in men's hearts surrounded with selfishness and hatred and jealousy and malignance and envy and strife, if treachery and greed and ingratitude are mixed in the sacred chalice, if grossness of passion and unrefined desire degrade devotion, in such hearts the gracious and beautiful Goddess will not linger. A divine disgust seizes upon her, and she withdraws, for she is not one who insists or strives; or, veiling her face, she waits for this bitter and poisonous devil's stuff to be rejected and disappear before she will find anew her happy influence. Ascetic bareness and harshness are not pleasing to her nor the suppression of the heart's deeper emotions and the rigid repression of the soul's and the life's parts of beauty. For it is through love and beauty that she lays on men the yoke of the Divine. Life is turned in her supreme creations into a rich work of celestial art and all existence into a poem of sacred delight; the world's riches are brought together and concerted for a supreme order and even the simplest and commonest things are made wonderful by her intuition of unity and the breath of her spirit. Admitted to the heart she lifts wisdom to pinnacles of wonder and reveals to it the mystic secrets of the ecstasy that surpasses all knowledge, meets devotion with the passionate attraction of the Divine, teaches to strength and force the rhythm that keeps the might of their acts harmonious and in measure and casts on perfection the charm that makes it endure forever.

MAHASARASWATI is the Mother's Power of Work and her spirit of perfection and order. The youngest of the Four, she is the most skillful in executive faculty and the nearest to physical Nature. Maheshwari lays down the large lines of the world-forces, Mahakali drives their energy and impetus, Mahalakshmi discovers their rhythms and measures, but Mahasaraswati presides over their detail of organisation and execution, relation of parts and effective combination of forces and unfailing exactitude of result and fulfilment. The science and craft and technique of things are Mahasaraswati's province. Always she holds in her nature and can give to those whom she has chosen the intimate and precise knowledge, the subtlety and patience, the accuracy of intuitive mind and conscious hand and discerning eye of the perfect worker. This Power is the strong, the tireless, the careful and efficient builder, organiser, administrator, technician, artisan and classifier of the worlds. When she takes up the transformation and new-building of the nature, her action is laborious and minute and often seems to our impatience slow and interminable, but it is persistent, integral and flawless. For the will in her works is scrupulous, unsleeping, indefatigable; leaning over us she notes and touches every little detail, finds out every minute defect, gap, twist or incompleteness, considers and weighs accurately all that has been done and all that remains still to be done hereafter. Nothing is too small or apparently trivial for her attention; nothing however impalpable or disguised or latent can escape her. Moulding and remoulding she labours each part till it has attained its true form, is put in its exact place in the whole and fulfils its precise purpose. In her constant and diligent arrangement and rearrangement of things her eye is on all needs at once and the way to meet them and her intuition knows what is to be chosen and what rejected and successfully determines the right instrument, the right time, the right conditions and the right process. Carelessness and negligence and indolence she abhors; all scamped and hasty and shuffling work, all clumsiness and *à peu près* and misfire, all false adaptation and misuse of instruments and faculties and leaving of things undone or half done is offensive and foreign to her temper. When her work is finished, nothing has been forgotten, no part has been misplaced or omitted or left in a faulty condition; all is solid, accurate, complete, admirable. Nothing short of a perfect perfection satisfies her and she is ready to face an eternity of toil if that is needed for the fullness of her creation. Therefore, of all the Mother's powers she is the most long-suffering with man and his thousand imperfections. Kind, smiling, close and helpful, not easily turned away or discouraged, insistent even after repeated failure, her hand sustains our every step on condition that we are single in our will and straightforward and sincere; for a double mind she will not tolerate, and her revealing irony is merciless to drama and histrionics and self-deceit and pretence. A mother to our wants, a friend in our difficulties, a persistent and tranquil counsellor and mentor, chasing away with her radiant smile the clouds of gloom and fretfulness and depression, reminding always of the ever-present help, pointing to the eternal sunshine, she is firm, quiet and persevering in the deep and continuous urge that drives us towards the integrality of the higher nature. All the work of the other Powers leans on her for its completeness; for she assures the material foundation, elaborates the stuff of detail and erects and rivets the armour of the structure.

There are other great Personalities of the Divine Mother, but they were more difficult to bring down and have not stood out in front with so much prominence in the evolution of the earth-spirit. There are among them Presences indispensable for the supramental realisation, — most of all one who is her Personality of that mysterious and powerful ecstasy and Ananda which flows from a supreme divine

Love, the Ananda that alone can heal the gulf between the highest heights of the supramental spirit and the lowest abysses of Matter, the Ananda that holds the key of a wonderful divinest Life and even now supports from its secrecies the work of all the other Powers of the universe. But human nature bounded, egoistic and obscure is inapt to receive these great Presences or to support their mighty action. Only when the Four have founded their harmony and freedom of movement in the transformed mind and life and body, can those other rarer Powers manifest in the earth movement and the supramental action become possible. For when her Personalities are all gathered in her and manifested and their separate working has been turned into a harmonious unity and they rise in her to their supramental godheads, then is the Mother revealed as the supramental Mahashakti and brings pouring down her luminous transcendences from their ineffable ether. Then can human nature change into dynamic divine nature because all the elemental lines of the supramental Truth-consciousness and Truth-force are strung together, and the harp of life is fitted for the rhythms of the Eternal.

If you desire this transformation, put yourself in the hands of the Mother and her Powers without cavil or resistance and let her do unhindered her work within you. Three things you must have, consciousness, plasticity, unreserved surrender. For you must be conscious in your mind and soul and heart and life and the very cells of your body, aware of the Mother and her Powers and their working; for although she can and does work in you even in your obscurity and your unconscious parts and moments, it is not the same thing as when you are in an awakened and living communion with her. All your nature must be plastic to her touch, — not questioning as the self-sufficient ignorant mind questions and doubts and disputes and is the enemy of its enlightenment and change; not insisting on its own movements as the vital in man insists and persistently opposes its refractory desires and ill-will to every divine influence; not obstructing and entrenched in incapacity, inertia and tamas as man's physical consciousness obstructs and clinging to its pleasure in smallness and darkness cries out against each touch that disturbs its soulless routine or its dull sloth or its torpid slumber. The unreserved surrender of your inner and outer being will bring this plasticity into all the parts of your nature; consciousness will awaken everywhere in you by constant openness to the Wisdom and Light, the Force, the Harmony and Beauty, the Perfection that come flowing down from above. Even the body will awake and unite at last its consciousness subliminal no longer to the supramental superconscious Force, feel all her powers permeating from above and below and around it and thrill to a supreme Love and Ananda.

But be on your guard and do not try to understand and judge the Divine Mother by your little earthly mind that loves to subject even the things that are beyond it to its own norms and standards, its narrow reasonings and erring impressions, its bottomless aggressive ignorance and its petty self-confident knowledge. The human mind shut in the prison of its half-lit obscurity cannot follow the many-sided freedom of the steps of the Divine Shakti. The rapidity and complexity of her vision and action outrun its stumbling comprehension; the measures of her movement are not its measures. Bewildered by the swift alternation of her many different personalities, her making of rhythms and her breaking of rhythms, her accelerations of speed and her retardations, her varied ways of dealing with the problem of one and of another, her taking up and dropping now of this line and now of that one and her gathering of them together, it will not recognise the way of the Supreme Power when it is circling and sweeping upwards through the maze of the Ignorance to a supernal Light. Open rather your soul to her and be content to feel her with the psychic nature and see her with the psychic vision that alone make a straight response to the Truth. Then the Mother herself will enlighten by their psychic elements your mind and heart and life and physical consciousness and reveal to them too her ways and her nature.

Avoid also the error of the ignorant mind's demand on the Divine Power to act always according to our crude surface notions of omniscience and omnipotence. For our mind clamours to be impressed at every turn by miraculous power and easy success and dazzling splendour; otherwise, it cannot believe that here is the Divine. The Mother is dealing with the Ignorance in the fields of the Ignorance; she has descended there and is not all above. Partly she veils and partly she unveils her knowledge and her power, often holds them back from her instruments and personalities and follows that she may transform them the way of the seeking mind, the way of the aspiring psychic, the way of the battling vital, the way of the imprisoned and suffering physical nature. There are conditions that have been laid down by a Supreme Will, there are many tangled knots that have to be loosened and cannot be cut abruptly asunder. The Asura and Rakshasa hold this evolving earthly nature and have to be met and conquered on their own terms in their own long-conquered fief and province; the human in us has to be led and prepared to transcend its limits and is too weak and obscure to be lifted up suddenly to a form far beyond it. The Divine Consciousness and Force are there and do at each moment the thing that is needed in the conditions of the labour, take always the step that is decreed and shape in the midst of imperfection the perfection that is to come. But only when the super-mind has descended in you can she deal directly as the supramental Shakti with supramental natures. If you follow your mind, it will not recognise the Mother even when she is manifest before you. Follow your soul and not your mind, your soul that answers to the Truth, not your mind that leaps at appearances; trust the Divine Power and she will free the godlike elements in you and shape all into an expression of Divine Nature.

The supramental change is a thing decreed and inevitable in the evolution of the earth-consciousness; for its upward ascent is not ended and mind is not its last summit. But that the change may arrive, take form and endure, there is needed the call from below with a will to recognise and not deny the Light when it comes, and there is needed the sanction of the Supreme from above. The power that mediates between the sanction and the call is the presence and power of the Divine Mother. The Mother's power and not any human endeavour and Tapasya can alone rend the lid and tear the covering and shape the vessel and bring down into this world of obscurity and falsehood and death and suffering Truth and Light and Life divine and the immortal's Ananda.